My First Pocket Guide

CONNECTICUT

By Carole Marsh

Correlates with Connecticut's™ CCL Common Core of Learning

THE CONNECTICUT Experience™

The GALLOPADE GANG

Carole Marsh
Bob Longmeyer
Chad Beard
Cecil Anderson
Steven Saint-Laurent
Karin Petersen
Billie Walburn
Doug Boston
Jill Sanders
William Nesbitt, Jr.
Kathy Zimmer
Wanda Coats
Terry Briggs
Jackie Clayton
Pam Dufresne
Cranston Davenport
Lisa Stanley
Antoinette Miller
Victoria DeJoy

Published by GALLOPADE INTERNATIONAL

www.connecticutexperience.com
800-536-2GET • www.gallopade.com

A Word From the Author... (okay, a few words)...

Hi!

Here's your own handy pocket guide about the great state of Connecticut! It really will fit in a pocket–I tested it. And it really will be useful when you want to know a fact you forgot, to bone up for a test, or when your teacher says, "I wonder . . ." and you have the answer–instantly! Wow, I'm impressed!

Get smart, have fun!

Carole Marsh

Connecticut Basics explores your state's symbols and their special meanings!

Connecticut Geography digs up the what's where in your state!

Connecticut History is like traveling through time to some of your state's great moments!

Connecticut People introduces you to famous personalities and your next-door neighbors!

Connecticut Places shows you where you might enjoy your next family vacation!

Connecticut Nature - no preservatives here, just what Mother Nature gave to Connecticut!

All the real fun stuff that we just HAD to save for its own section!

Who Named You?

Connecticut's official state name is...

Connecticut

State Name

Word Definition

OFFICIAL: appointed, authorized, or approved by a government or organization

Statehood: January 9, 1788

Connecticut was the 5th state to join the United States.

What's In A Name?

Connecticut's name came from the Algonquian word, *Quinnehtukqut*, which means "long river place" or "beside the tidal river."

Who Are You Calling Names?

State Nicknames

Like many other states, Connecticut has some nicknames, official and unofficial!

Connecticut got its official nickname of the Constitution State because its Fundamental Orders, or rules by which the colony governed itself, was America's first constitution.

Folks from Connecticut have been called practical—and even predictable—which makes Connecticut the Land of Steady Habits!

The Nutmeg State is one of Connecticut's best-known nicknames, but it's not necessarily the nicest. This refers to rather shady business dealings of salesmen selling the spice nutmeg. Sometimes they would carve wood into nutmeg shapes and peddle them off as the real thing!

Connecticut is known as the **Provisions State** because it provided supplies for the army during the American Revolution.

Hartford

From 1701 to 1875, Connecticut had two capitals—New Haven and Hartford.

Connecticut's state capitol features a beautiful gold dome that can be seen from all over Hartford. The building was completed in 1879. It houses offices for the legislative and executive branches of government.

Visitors to the Connecticut capitol building can take a tour to see sculptures and carved scenes throughout. Some statues are of people who were significant during the Revolutionary War. One of these people is Connecticut native Nathan Hale. He was convicted and hanged for being a spy for the Americans during the war.

The first *tympana*, or carved scene, to be created for the capitol was a replica of the state's signature tree, the Charter Oak. Its prominent position in the center of the capitol lets visitors know its importance to the state's heritage.

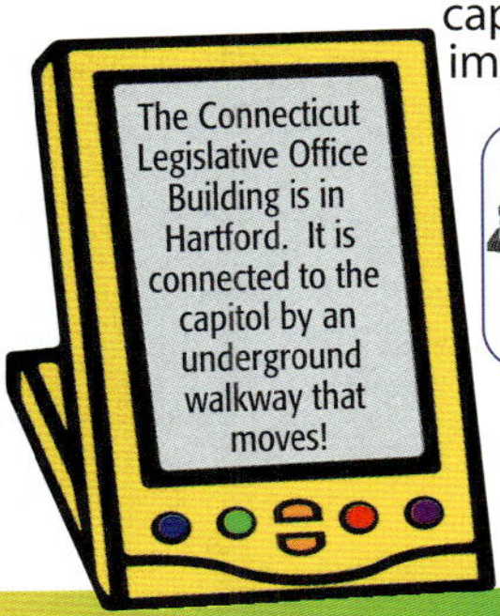

Word Definition

CAPITAL: a town or city that is the official seat of government

CAPITOL: the building in which the government officials meet

Who's in Charge Here?

Connecticut's GOVERNMENT has three branches:

- **LEGISLATIVE**
  - *The legislative branch is called the General Assembly.*
  - Two Houses: THE SENATE (36 members); HOUSE OF REPRESENTATIVES (151 members)
- **EXECUTIVE**
  - Governor, lieutenant governor, secretary of state, attorney general, state treasurer, state comptroller
- **JUDICIAL**
  - SUPREME COURT (six justices) over the Appellate Court, Superior Court, and Probate Courts

Connecticut's 169 towns have their own governments. Many of the towns still hold annual town meetings where citizens can stand up and voice their concerns and vote for new officials.

State Flag

State Flag

Connecticut's state flag was adopted in 1897.

Connecticut's state flag has an official size: 5 feet 6 inches by 4 feet 4 inches (1.6 by 1.3 meters). The state coat of arms and motto are featured on the flag's azure silk background.

State Seal & Motto

State Seal

Connecticut's state seal features three grapevines that symbolize the three original Connecticut River towns (Hartford, Windsor, and Wethersfield) which were settled by colonists from Massachusetts. The three grapevines are also said to represent the three European cultures of the French, Dutch, and English, who first lived in the colony.

State Seal & Motto

Word Definition

MOTTO: a sentence, phrase, or word expressing the spirit or purpose of an organization or group

State Motto

Connecticut's state motto is... *Qui transtulit sustinet*

This translates from Latin into English as "He who transplanted still sustains."

American Robin

New England states like Connecticut are often where robins choose to roost during the Winter. They seem especially fond of evergreen trees in swampy areas. Winter berries serve as food for the red-chested Winter guests.

The Robin was named Connecticut's state bird in 1943.

White Oak

Connecticut's state tree is the White Oak. This is probably the best known of all oak trees and is common throughout New England.

Acorns are the White Oak's seeds. They are larger than acorns from other varieties of the oak and have shallow cups. The Indians used White Oak acorns as a food source.

White Oaks grow very slowly, but can grow to be very tall—up to 120 feet (36 meters). The White Oak is known for its sturdy lumber. It's used to build furniture, boats, and barrels.

Connecticut has a famous White Oak known as the Charter Oak. To learn more about it, keep reading and check out the legend on page 41.

Mountain Laurel

The Mountain Laurel has been described as the most beautiful of native American flowering shrubs. John Smith mentioned the blossoms in his "General History" in 1624.

In full bloom, this bush looks like a small tree covered in snowballs, but new blossoms can be deep pink. In late June, the Connecticut countryside is spotted with "snowdrifts" of Mountain Laurel. This plant is also known as the Calico Bush or Spoonwood.

State Animal

Sperm Whale

In the 1800s, whaling was an important industry in Connecticut. In fact, Sperm Whales are almost extinct because of over-hunting. However, efforts are now being made to increase their numbers.

Large male Sperm Whales can be up to 60 feet (18.2 meters) long. Females, known as cows, are usually about half that long. Sperm Whales sometimes dive as deep as 1 mile (1.61 kilometers), where they hunt for food, mainly giant squid and cuttlefish. Sperm Whales eat around 1 ton (0.91 metric ton) of food each day! Perhaps giant squid and cuttlefish can be considered "brain food" since the Sperm Whale has the largest brain of any known living creature.

In 1975 the Sperm Whale was named the Connecticut state animal.

RIDDLE: What do you get when you cross the state bird with the state animal?

ANSWER: A whale of a songbird!

Garnet

Garnets are prized by jewelry makers for their rich violet-red color, but they can also be pale in color. Not only is Garnet beautiful in jewelry, it is valuable to many Connecticut industries. This hard mineral is used as an abrasive to grind wheels, saws, and for making high-quality sandpaper.

The violet-red variety of Garnets are known as almandine Garnets. Connecticut has one of the best supplies in the world!

Saint Albertus Magnus was the first person to note the Garnet. In the 13th century he called it the "garnata." Six hundred years later, in 1977, the Connecticut General Assembly named Garnet the state mineral.

To see examples of Connecticut Garnets and even some from around the world, visit the Connecticut State Museum of Natural History at Storrs.

Eastern Oyster

Connecticut's coast off Long Island Sound makes a great place for harvesting Eastern Oysters. Oysters are members of the bivalve family, which means they have two shells, joined at the back by a hinge.

Oysters are known for producing pearls. This happens when a grain of sand gets inside the oyster shell and irritates the sea creature. The oyster begins covering the grain with layers and layers of shiny, smooth material. Eventually after the layers build up, the sand grain becomes a pearl.

Oysters are used as food more often than any other bivalve. Oyster stew is a popular way to enjoy the Connecticut state shellfish. Here's a recipe you can try. Hey kids, be sure to get help from an adult.

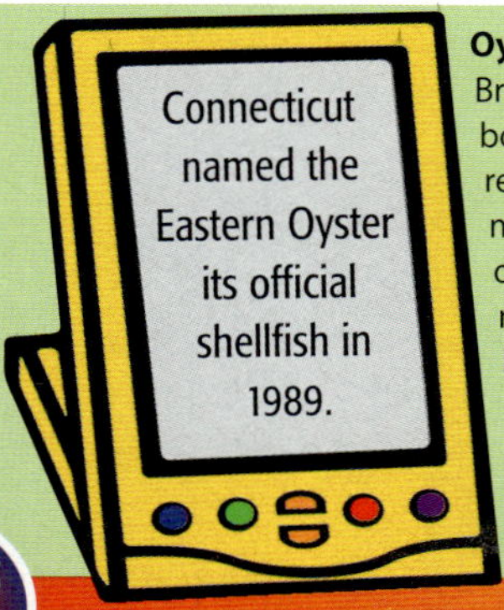

Oyster Stew

Bring 2 cups of milk to a boil over medium heat; reduce heat and keep warm. In another medium saucepan, cook 1 pint select oysters and their liquid for 3 to 5 minutes until the edges of the oysters begin to curl. Add the warm milk. Add 1 1/2 tablespoons butter, and stir to melt butter. Season to taste with salt and pepper. Serve with oyster crackers or regular saltines.

USS *Nautilus*

Connecticut's state ship is a submarine. This state can claim the fame of being where the first nuclear-powered submarine was built. The USS *Nautilus* was built and launched in Groton in 1954. It was designated as the state ship in 1983.

Today it has been converted into a museum and is listed as a National Historic Landmark. It has been permanently berthed, or "parked," in Groton, next to the Submarine Force Library.

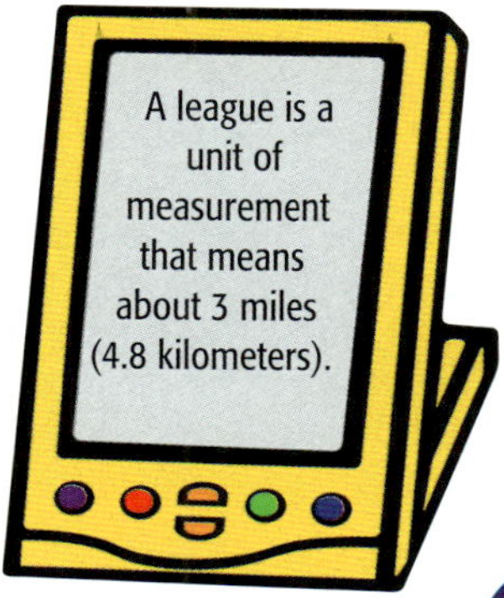

Nathan Hale

"I regret that I have but one life to lose for my country," Nathan Hale is quoted as saying before he was hanged by the British for being an American spy during the Revolutionary War. Hale was a schoolteacher who was one of the first teachers in America to offer classes to young ladies as well as young men. Hale was captured when he was only 21 years old and he is remembered for his bravery and eloquence.

Prudence Crandall

Another important figure in Connecticut's history is state heroine Prudence Crandall. Like Nathan Hale, she recognized that women were just as worthy of education as men. In 1833, she opened a school for young black women in Canterbury. However, her school was attacked by a mob of townspeople who were outraged by the idea of a school for African Americans in their community. Fearing for the safety of her students, she closed the school. Today, her home is a museum of local and African-American women's history.

State Composer and Folk Dance

Charles Ives is the state composer for Connecticut. He was born in 1874 in Danbury and died in 1954. He made his living as an insurance salesman rather than as a composer. In 1947, Ives won the Pulitzer Prize in music for his *Third Symphony*. Ives' music was more popular in Europe than in America, perhaps because his music is not considered "pretty." It's even been called "grand and glorious noise," but this didn't bother him. Today, many people enjoy listening to the music of Connecticut's state composer, Charles Ives!

Charles Ives' music might not be the right music for the state folk dance, the **Square Dance**, which relies more on a definite rhythm. The Square Dance is an American folk dance which traces its roots to the English country dance and the French ballroom dance. The Square Dance comes in many other shapes, too, including rounds and lines and clogging and reels.

European Mantis

The European Mantis is more commonly known as the Praying Mantis. Often this insect looks like it is "standing" on its hind legs with its front legs drawn up like it is praying, and maybe it is—for food. The Mantis is well-liked by farmers because it eats harmful pests such as flies, caterpillars, grasshoppers, aphids, and moths. The European Mantis is not native to Connecticut, but it can be found all over the state.

The State of Connecticut

State Map

State Location

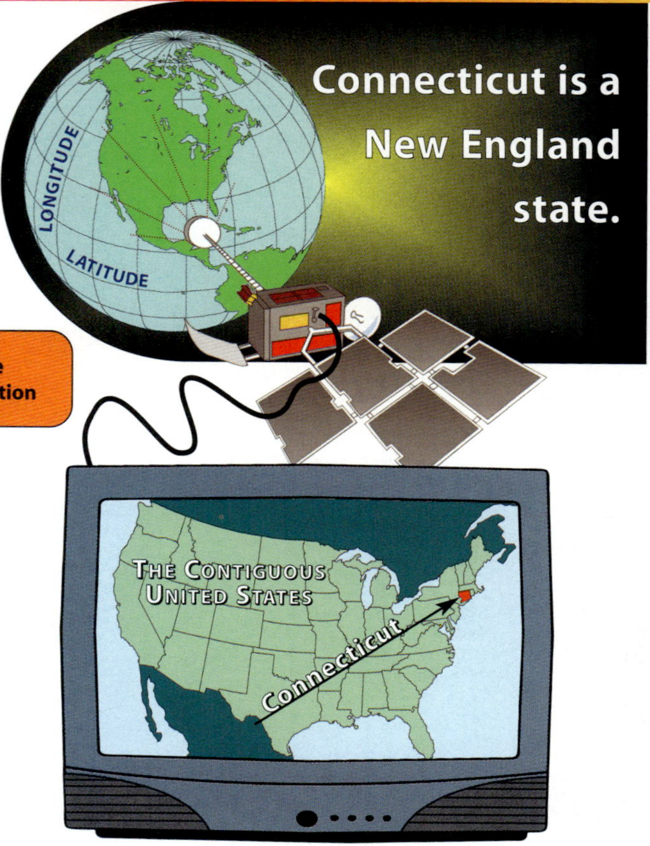

State Location

Word Definition

LATITUDE: Imaginary lines which run horizontally east and west around the globe
LONGITUDE: Imaginary lines which run vertically north and south around the globe

On The Border!

These border Connecticut:

States: New York

Massachusetts

Rhode Island

Bodies of water: Long Island Sound

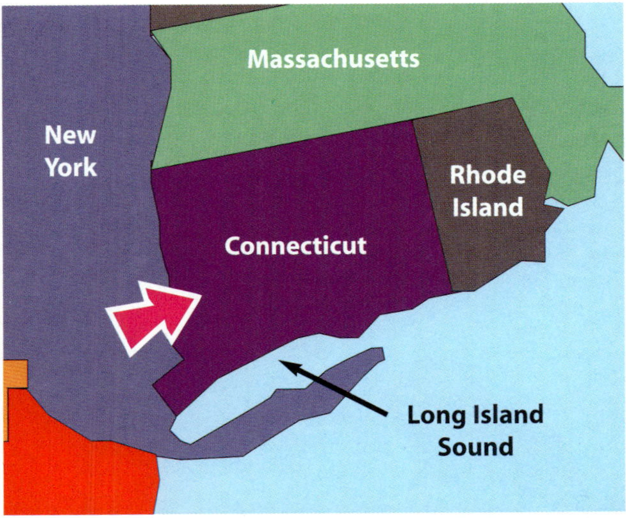

I'll Take the Low Road...

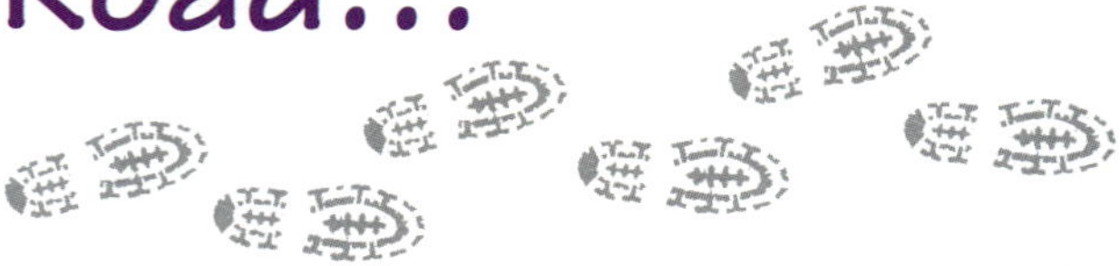

Connecticut is 101 miles (163 kilometers) from east to west—or west to east. Either way, it's a long walk!

Total Area: 5,544 square miles (14,359 square kilometers)

Land Area: 4,845 square miles (12,548 square kilometers)

Connecticut is 73 miles (117 kilometers) from north to south—or south to north. Either way, it's still a long walk!

You Take the High Road!

Highest Point

Mount Frissell—2,380 feet (725 meters)

While the 2,380-foot figure is the highest point in Connecticut, Mount Frissell's peak is actually on the Massachusetts side. The highest mountaintop entirely in Connecticut is Bear Mountain, at 2,316 feet (706 meters).

The Appalachian Trail hikes through 51 miles (82 kilometers) of Connecticut near both Mount Frissell and Bear Mountain. You can hike up Mount Frissell, too, but be aware that the primary route has a "Private Property—No Trespassing" sign posted; however, hikers are allowed to get on the trail there.

Lowest Point

Sea Level, along Long Island Sound

I'm County-ing on You!

Connecticut is divided into eight counties: Fairfield, Hartford, Litchfield, Middlesex, New Haven, New London, Tolland, and Windham.

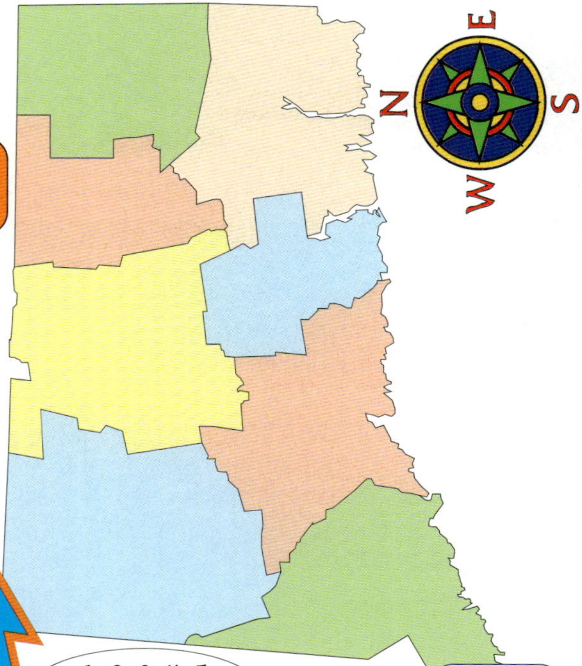

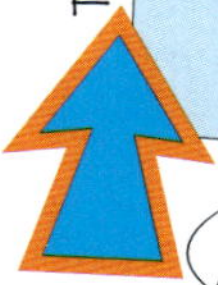

Word Definition

COUNTY: an administrative subdivision of a state or territory

It's All Natural!

Word Definition

NATURAL RESOURCES: things that exist in or are formed by nature

Natural Resources:

Clay
Granite
Limestone
Mica
Crushed Stone
Sand

Settlers in Connecticut soon learned that the land was not good for farming because most of it is hilly or rocky. They found other methods to make a living including manufacturing, particularly in metalworks, and in the sales industry.

Deep-water Ports:
New Haven, Bridgeport, New London

Weather, Or Not?!

Connecticut enjoys four distinct seasons. Trees and shrubs (including the state flower Mountain Laurel) bud and blossom in the Spring. Fields and gardens "green up" during the Summer. The state's hardwood trees are brilliantly colored in the Fall, and Winter turns areas of Connecticut into a postcard-perfect wonderland.

Highest temperature: 105°F (41°C) at Waterbury on July 22, 1926

°F=Degrees Fahrenheit °C=Degrees Celsius

Lowest temperature: -32°F (-36°C) at Falls Village on February 16, 1943

In 1936 and again in 1955, Connecticut experienced heavy flooding. In the flood of 1955, 164 bridges and more than 176 miles (283 kilometers) of roads were damaged or destroyed.

BACK ON TOP

Connecticut's topography consists of five main land areas:
NORTHWEST: The Taconic Mountains
SOUTH: Coastal Lowland
WEST: Heavy forests, rocky hills
CENTRAL: Level terrain mixed with rolling hills
EAST: Rolling land with narrow valleys and low hills

Connecticut is home to salt marshes, but these have changed since prehistoric times due to the influence of humans. Connecticut conservationists are hoping the marshes will return to their original state one day.

In prehistoric times, Indian tribes settled nearby because of the marshes' food offerings. During the colonial period, marshland was drained to create more farmland. The flow of water in the lowlands was also changed sometimes to create ponds for mills.

Wetlands and their inhabitants have also been endangered as humans built bridges and causeways. These changes altered the tide patterns. Even attempts to control disease-carrying mosquitos have had effects because ditches were dug to keep water from standing and becoming mosquito factories. Today, the idea of ditches has been ditched!

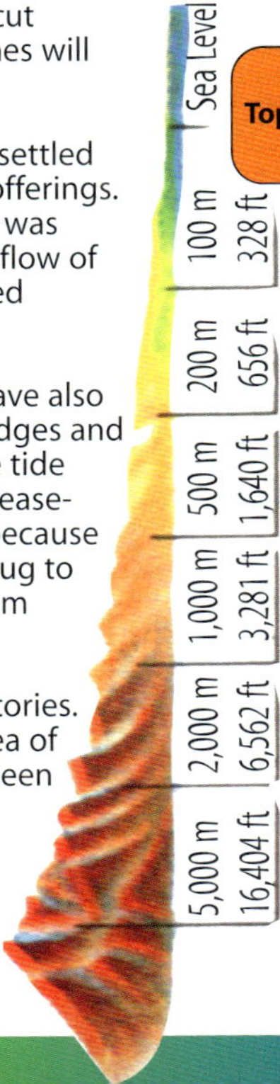

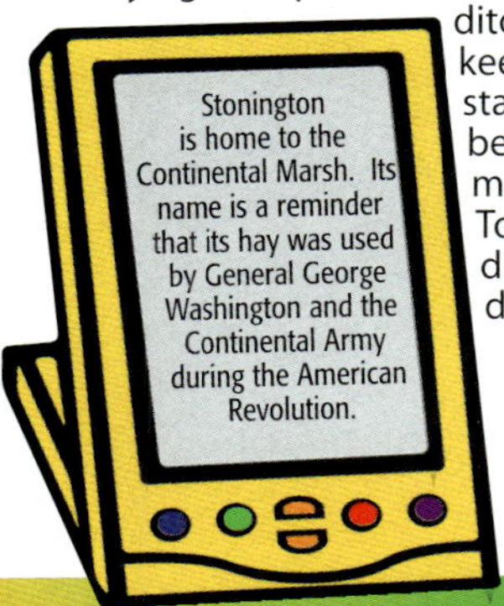

King of the Hill

The Taconic Mountains barely reach into Connecticut. Mount Frissell is the highest point in the state and its peak is not even in Connecticut.

Other mountains include:

- Bear Mountain
- Gridley Mountain
- Canaan Mountain
- Ball Mountain
- Haystack Mountain
- Tom Mountain
- Titus Mountain
- Red Mountain

Connecticut is also home to a number of hills, including:

- Cream Hill
- Dennis Hill

Major Rivers

A River Runs Through It!

The Connecticut River cuts through central Connecticut. Sailors can navigate 50 miles (80 kilometers) inland to Hartford on the Connecticut. In all, the state has about 8,400 miles (13,518 kilometers) of rivers.

Here are some of Connecticut's major rivers:

- **Housatonic**
- **Quinebaug**
- **Thames**
- **Naugatuck**

Connecticut has a few small islands, including the Thimbles, offshore in Long Island Sound.

Gone Fishin'

Lake Candlewood
Bantam Lake

Major Lakes

Lake Candlewood is the largest man-made lake, or reservoir in Connecticut. It covers 9 square miles (23 square kilometers).

Long Island Sound is never farther than 75 miles (120 kilometers) from anywhere in Connecticut.

Word Definition

RESERVOIR: a body of water stored for public use

ARE YOU A COUNTRY MOUSE... OR CITY MOUSE?

Have you heard of these wonderful Connecticut town, city, or crossroad names? Perhaps you can start your own list!

LARGER TOWNS:

Bridgeport
Hartford
New Haven
Waterbury
Stamford
Norwalk
New Britain
West Hartford
Danbury
Greenwich
Falls Village

SMALLER TOWNS:

Boardmans Bridge
Dayville
Derby
Hazardville
Moosup
Honeypot Glen
Huckleberry Hill
Indian Neck
Moodus
Mystic
Prospect
Rainbow
Sandy Hook
Yantic

Transportation

Major Interstate Highways

I-95, I-84, I-91

Connecticut has about 20,571 miles (33,105 kilometers) of roads and highways.

Transpor-tation

Railroads

About 45 Connecticut cities have passenger train service. Four railroads transport freight.

The Hartford and New Haven was the first railroad line in Connecticut. It began service in 1838.

Major Airports

Bradley International Airport in Windsor Locks is the international airport in Connecticut.

Seaports

About 20 million tons (18 million metric tons) of cargo pass through the three main ports of Bridgeport, New Haven, and New London each year.

Timeline

- 1614 Adriaen Block explores and claims area for Holland
- 1633 English settle in Windsor, Dutch colonize Hartford
- 1636 Windsor, Wethersfield, and Hartford unite to form colony
- 1637 Settlers defeat Pequot Indians
- 1638 Colony of New Haven (at Quinnipiac) established
- 1639 Connecticut Colony adopts Fundamental Orders
- 1654 English drive Dutch from state
- 1707 Copper first mined in America at Simsbury Mine
- 1765 Sons of Liberty formed after England passes Stamp Act
- 1775 Litchfield native Ethan Allen captures Fort Ticonderoga
- 1776 Connecticut declares independence from Great Britain, Great Britain executes Nathan Hale for being a spy
- 1788 Connecticut joins Union as fifth state
- 1839 Charles Goodyear discovers method to vulcanize rubber
- 1881 Connecticut and New York finally agree on state border
- 1943 Connecticut first to create a civil rights commission
- 1965 Connecticut adopts current state constitution
- 1974 Ella Grasso elected first female governor of Connecticut
- 1982 Appellate Court created by constitutional amendment
- 1990 Eunice S. Groark elected first female lieutenant governor of Connecticut

On to the 21st century!

Here come the humans!

Thousands of years ago, ancient peoples came to the area that would one day be the state of Connecticut. They may have originally come across a frozen bridge of land which once connected Asia and Alaska. The Paleo-Indians became the ancestors of Connecticut's Native American population.

Native Americans Once Ruled!

Connecticut's early Indians were all a part of the large Algonquian-speaking family. They were divided into four main groups who frequently fought among themselves and were never able to unite against common enemies. A group of tribes, the Matabesecs, lived in the hills of western Connecticut. Another confederation, the Sequins, made their home along the Connecticut River. The Nipmuc were a peaceful people who lived in the forests of northeastern Connecticut. The powerful Pequots called the forest of the southeast home, sweet home!

Word Definition

WAMPUM: beads, pierced and strung, used by Indians as money, or for ornaments or ceremonies.

Land Ho!

In the 1500s and 1600s, French, Dutch, and English explorers sailed along the coast and up and down the rivers of Canada and America. They found a beautiful, bountiful land of opportunity. News of the New World traveled fast—although not as fast as it would today—and brought more Europeans looking for new lands, natural resources, and a place where they could freely worship God.

In 1614, Adriaen Block of Holland sailed his ship, the *Restless,* up the Connecticut River. Block and his Dutch crew were the first Europeans to explore Connecticut. They sent word of America back to Holland and told of forests alive with beavers and other fur-bearing animals!

Fur trading companies hired boatmen called *voyageurs* to transport furs and supplies along the waterways of the colonies.

Home, Sweet Home

In 1633, William Holmes traveled from the English colony of Massachusetts Bay and established a trading post at present-day Windsor. In 1633, John Oldham, another colonist from Massachusetts Bay, explored the Connecticut Valley. In 1634, he led a small party into the Connecticut wilderness. They established a settlement on the site of present-day Wethersfield.

Thomas Hooker, a Puritan clergyman, is considered the founder of Connecticut. In 1636, he led a small group of parishioners, along with their cows and pigs, on a two-week journey from their homes in the Massachusetts Bay Colony to their brand-new homes at a settlement in Connecticut named Hartford. Thomas Hooker became the colony's spiritual and political leader.

The Colony of Connecticut was created as a *theocracy* by the Puritans. A theocracy is a community that's governed by the church.

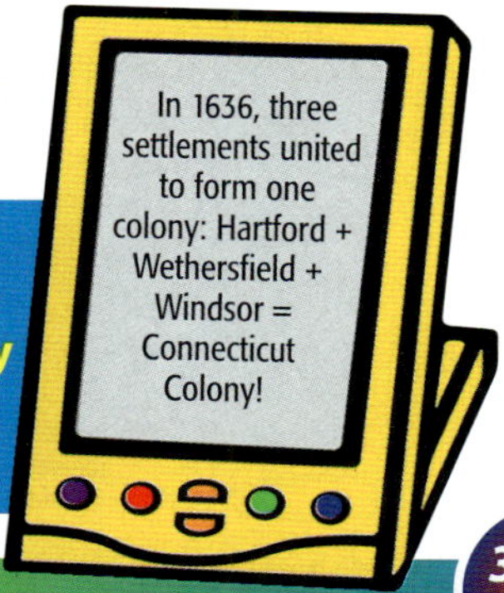

One for the Bug!

In early days, colonists were mostly self-sufficient. They cleared their lands, built their homes and furnishings, grew crops, and made their own clothing. Neighbors helped neighbors. They grew rye, oats, peas, squash, turnips, onions, tobacco, and of course—corn, then known as maize.

Have you ever thought about being a farmer? In colonial days, farming could be difficult and frustrating. Back then, farmers had a saying about the corn crop: "One for the bug and one for the crow, one to rot and two to grow."

When colonists needed things they couldn't grow, make, or build, they went shopping. They bought imported goods such as molasses, spices, glassware, and gunpowder from local shopkeepers in nearby towns.

Charter Oak

The Charter Oak was a beautiful oak tree in Hartford that was very special to Native Americans and Connecticut colonists. Native Americans believed the Great Spirit sent them a sign each spring through the blooms on the tree telling them when the time was right to plant corn.

The oak tree played an important role for the colonists, as well. In 1687, Sir Edmund Andros arrived in Hartford to demand that the Connecticut Colony Charter be handed over. King Charles II of England had issued the charter which allowed the colony to be mostly independent. Charles was now dead and the new king, James II, wanted the charter and the colony back!

During a meeting discussing the charter, someone blew out the lamps, and someone else grabbed the charter, ran, and stashed it in the old oak. The charter remained hidden until Andros no longer posed a threat! The tree became known as the Charter Oak and stood as a symbol of Connecticut's freedom.

The Charter Oak was destroyed by a storm in 1856, but lives on in the hearts of all Connecticut citizens. The tree's beloved image is carved on the capitol building in Hartford.

Freedom!

The Stamp Act of 1765 required colonial newspapers, legal documents, licenses, and even playing cards to carry a stamp sold by the British government. The Sons of Liberty was formed by Eliphalet Dyer and Jonathan Trumbull to protest the new tax. The British government got the message loud and clear and repealed the tax in 1766. The Sons of Liberty movement was the beginning of the fight for American independence!

The American Revolution started in 1775. The colonists fought tirelessly and bravely year after year. England finally surrendered in 1781 at Yorktown, Virginia. In 1783, England signed a peace treaty recognizing colonial independence. The United States of America was born!

In 1781, about 150 American soldiers at Fort Griswold held off 800 British troops, until they were defeated by a British bayonet charge. Eighty Americans were killed by the battle's end.

Of Human Bondage

Although some families owned slaves during the colonial period, slavery was never widespread in Connecticut. The years following the American Revolution brought a gradual end to the cruel practice in the state. By 1848, the last 20 slaves in Connecticut were set free.

Connecticut was involved in a famous legal case about a Spanish slave ship named the *Amistad*. In 1839, the ship was seen drifting in Long Island Sound. The Africans who had been captured and forced to board the *Amistad* revolted and took over the ship in hopes of returning home. Spain tried to reclaim its "property," including the Africans, but compassionate Connecticut residents helped by hiring lawyers to plead the Africans' case for freedom. The Connecticut courts ruled in the Africans' favor. The U.S. Supreme Court upheld the decision and the surviving men, women, and children were finally allowed to sail back to their homes!

Many Connecticut men and women helped slaves escape to freedom in Canada on the Underground Railroad, a secret network of safe houses.

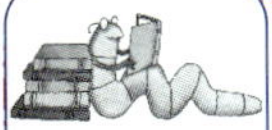

Word Definition

ABOLITIONIST: person who believed slavery was wrong and should be abolished.

The Civil War

Brother

The Civil War (1861-1865) was fought over slavery and the right of states to make their own individual decisions. The Confederacy, or Southern states, with plantations and slaves, were on one side of the conflict. The Union, or Northern states, opposed slavery or had no need for it, and were on the other side. Some states remained neutral.

The people of Connecticut enthusiastically supported the North. Within three days of President Abraham Lincoln's declaration of war on the South, the first regiment of volunteers was organized and ready for battle. As many as 50,000 Connecticut men joined the Union Army. Factories produced arms, ammunition, clothing, and other supplies that helped win the war!

On April 9, 1865, the Confederacy surrendered at Appomattox Court House in Virginia. It took years for the country to recover from the devastation of this unfortunate war, in which Americans could find no way to agree, except to fight.

Word Definition

RECONSTRUCTION: the recovery and rebuilding period following the Civil War.

vs. Brother

The Civil War was also called the War Between the States. Soldiers often found themselves fighting against former friends, neighbors, or family. Those who did survive often went home without an arm, leg, or both, since amputation was the "cure" for most battlefield wounds. More Americans were killed during the Civil War than during World Wars I and II together!

In 1863, the Emancipation Proclamation, issued by President Lincoln, freed the slaves in areas still under Confederate control.

Get It In Writing!

1639

Fundamental Orders, said to be the first "written" constitution

1662

Charter granted by England's King Charles II allowed much self-government in Connecticut

1776

Declaration of independence from England

1787

Connecticut delegates proposed the Great Compromise to allow all states to agree on a federal constitution. In 1788, Connecticut ratified the U.S. Constitution.

1965

Present state constitution adopted

Welcome to America!

People have come to Connecticut from other states and many other countries. As time has gone by, the state's population has grown more diverse. This means that people of different races and from different cultures and ethnic backgrounds have moved to Connecticut.

Early colonial residents of Connecticut originally came from Holland and England. More recently, people have come from Ireland, Poland, Italy, Germany, Greece, France, and Canada. Connecticut is proud of its ethnic heritage. The state's diverse population also includes people from Puerto Rico, Cambodia, Laos, Vietnam, Thailand, and Korea. Many of these immigrants eventually become U.S. citizens.

Disasters & Catastrophes!

1835

A devastating fire blazes through Manhattan, New York. The local insurance companies are overwhelmed and cannot reimburse clients for their damages. One insurance company in Hartford comes through and promptly pays clients for their losses. The Connecticut insurance companies win a reputation of reliability which continues today.

1888

The Great Blizzard roars through the Northeast killing hundreds of people with its ferocious winds, frigid temperatures, and blinding snow. The storm dumps tons of snow on Connecticut—up to 45 inches (114 centimeters) in New Haven! Drifts, hardened by high winds, are so big that people have to dig tunnels to get around on streets and sidewalks.

1936 & 1955

Massive flooding of Connecticut rivers kills hundreds of people and causes millions of dollars in damages. In 1936, areas along the Connecticut River, such as Hartford, are heavily damaged. The 1955 flood devastates lands along the Shetucket and Quinebaug rivers.

The first fire insurance company opened in Hartford in 1795. Today, Hartford is known as America's Insurance Capital with dozens of insurance companies headquartered there.

1938

A New England hurricane kills more than 600 people, blows down 275 million trees, and causes $250 million dollars in damages. This is the first hurricane to blast the area in more than 70 years.

Legal Stuff

1786

Connecticut cedes western lands, except Western Reserve, to U.S.

1936

A civil rights law passes which forbids discrimination based on "alienage, color, or race."

1943

Connecticut is first state to establish a civil rights commission.

1955

The legislature passes laws giving voters a direct choice in candidates running for state elections.

1979

Connecticut passes law banning new nuclear plant construction.

Women & Children

1650-1700

Connecticut is first colony to convict and hang a woman for practicing witchcraft; dozens of "witches" are tried and hanged

1650

Towns with 50 or more families required to hire a teacher to instruct children in reading and writing

1784

Connecticut frees all children born into slavery when they turn 25

1833

Prudence Crandall establishes an academy for young African-Americans

1975

Ella Grasso becomes first woman governor elected in her own right not to fill her husband's term

Fight! Fight! Fight!

Wars that had an impact on Connecticut:

- **The Pequot War of 1637**
- **King Philip's War**
- **French and Indian War**
- **American Revolution**
- **Civil War**
- **World War I**
- **World War II**
- **Korean War**
- **Vietnam War**
- **Persian Gulf War**

Claim to Fame

We have many claims to fame—not just one!
Read on and we'll tell you of some!

We were the first in 1639, you know,
to write a state constitution—it's so!

Innovators and great ideas are many!
Helpful inventions—we've invented plenty!

Guns, provisions, and ammunition we did supply!
For independence from England, our army to try!

If it's nutmeg you're after, buyer beware!
Those Yankee traders might give you a scare!

As the Land of Steady Habits we are known,
Proud, diligent, determined!
Press on, press on!

Indian Tribes

- Matabesecs (confederation of tribes)
- Sequins (confederation of tribes)
- Nipmuc
- Pequots
- Mohegans (tribe formed from Pequots by Chief Uncas)

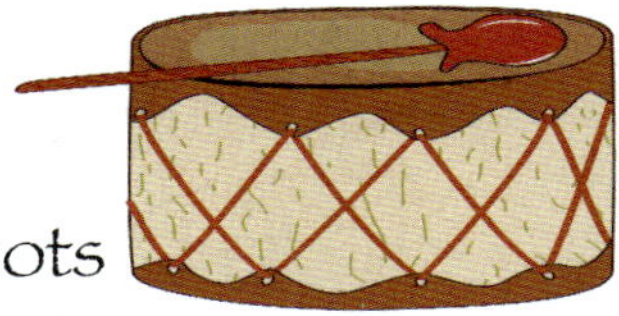

These Indians of Connecticut could not have known that the coming of the colonists would mean an end to the way of life they had known for hundreds of years!

Early Native Americans hunted deer, caught fish, and grew corn, beans, pumpkins, potatoes, tobacco, and squash. They moved from the forests to coastal areas as seasons changed. Frequently, whole villages moved.

Here, There, Everywhere!

Adriaen Block, a Dutch explorer, sailed up the Connecticut River with his crew in 1614. They were the first Europeans to set foot in Connecticut.

William Holmes was a colonist from Massachusetts Bay who explored the Connecticut Valley in 1633.

John Oldham was another colonist from Massachusetts Bay who explored the Connecticut Valley in 1633. In 1634, he led a small party into the Connecticut wilderness.

Hiram Bingham was an explorer who discovered the Incan ruins at Machu Picchu, in Peru, in 1911. He later became governor of Connecticut and a U.S. senator.

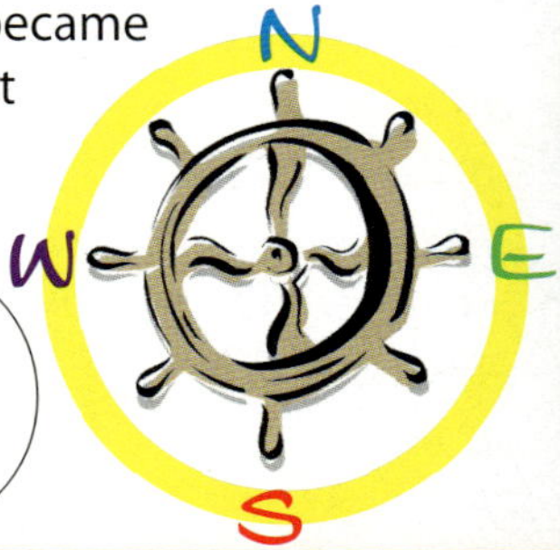

State Founders

These people played especially important roles in early Connecticut!

Founding Fathers

In 1638, Reverend John Davenport founded a colony at Quinnipiac, today's New Haven. More and more communities popped up in the New Haven Colony. Before long there were some coastal towns that even sounded alike—Guilford and Milford, Stamford and Branford.

Reverend Thomas Hooker is considered to be Connecticut's founder. In 1636, he led a group of Puritans from the Massachusetts Bay Colony into Connecticut where they established a community at Hartford. Reverend Hooker became the spiritual and political leader and was instrumental in creating the Fundamental Orders of 1639.

Founding Mothers

Catharine Esther Beecher was an educator who established a seminary for girls in Hartford. She was also the founder of the American Women's Educational Association.

Emma Willard was an educator and author who founded schools for young women in Connecticut and New York. She paved the way for women's high schools and colleges.

Famous Inventors

ELIAS HOWE—patented a sewing machine

CHARLES GOODYEAR—invented the vulcanizing process to prevent rubber from melting when heated

IGOR SIKORSKY—designed helicopters and multi-engine airplanes

EDWIN H. LAND—invented the Polaroid Land Camera and instant photography

ELI WHITNEY—invented the first cotton gin

SAMUEL COLT—created the first successful repeating pistol

CHARLES THURBER—invented the typewriter

G. C. BLICKENSDERFER—created the portable typewriter

ROBERT HALL—invented magnetron that operates most microwave ovens and the semiconductor laser used in compact disc players

IT WAS A WARM, SUMMER NIGHT IN WINDHAM CENTER, ABOUT 200 YEARS AGO.

Just after midnight, people were awakened by a loud, frightening noise! Some people thought that they were under attack by Indians. Others thought that the noise meant the world was coming to an end. Some people believed the noise was being made by a monster or a ghost. Everybody stayed inside, frightened, and waited for daylight.

After the long, loud night, people cautiously came out of their houses. One person yelled to the rest of them to come look at a strange sight. All around a small pond, there were hundreds of dead frogs! The pond had dried up during a recent drought. It looked like the frogs had been fighting with one another over what water remained! The battling frogs raised such a ruckus that it woke up the people in Windham Center! Since then, songs, poems, and even an operetta (small opera) were written about the mysterious fighting frogs of Windham Center!

Sports Figures

Famous Connecticut Sports Figures:

DOROTHY HAMILL—world champion ice skater, Olympic gold medalist

MO VAUGHN, ROGER CONNOR—professional baseball players

JULIUS BOROS—professional golfer

REBECCA LOBO—University of Connecticut basketball star; led the UConn Lady Huskies to an undefeated championship season

GORDIE HOWE—professional hockey player

CALVIN MURPHY—professional basketball player

JAMES "ORATOR JIM" O'ROURKE—professional baseball player, Hall of Famer; got the very first hit in National League

GEORGE WEISS—professional baseball executive, Hall of Famer

Performers

★ ERNEST BORGNINE, ED BEGLEY—actors, Academy Award winners

★ KAREN AND RICHARD CARPENTER—musicians, singers

★ GLENN CLOSE—actor, Tony Award winner

★ ROSALIND RUSSELL, LINDA EVANS—actors

★ MERYL STREEP, KATHARINE HEPBURN—actors, Academy Award winners

★ TED KNIGHT—actor, Emmy Award winner

★ PAUL NEWMAN AND JOANNE WOODWARD—husband and wife, Academy Award-winning actors

★ ROBERT MITCHUM—actor

?????? Which actor has food products named after him, and donates all of the profits to charity?

ANSWER: Paul Newman, Newman's Own Inc.

Authors

SAMUEL CLEMENS—author known as Mark Twain, beloved humorist; wrote *A Connecticut Yankee in King Arthur's Court, The Adventures of Tom Sawyer,* and *The Adventures of Huckleberry Finn*

CLARE BOOTH LUCE—playwright, politician, diplomat

MAURICE SENDAK—children's book author and illustrator; wrote *Where The Wild Things Are*

PETER De VRIES—author, playwright

WILLIAM HOOKER GILLETTE—playwright, actor

EUGENE O'NEILL—playwright; won Nobel Prize and Pulitzer Prizes

HARRIET BEECHER STOWE—author; wrote famous antislavery book titled *Uncle Tom's Cabin*

THOMAS TRYON—author, actor

NOAH WEBSTER—author, lexicographer; compiled the first major American dictionary

nom de plume: French for pen name, a fictitious name a writer chooses to write under instead of his/her real name

The Arts

JOHN TRUMBULL—artist; painted scenes from the American Revolution in small, dramatic paintings including *Battle of Bunker Hill* and *The Signing of the Declaration of Independence*

LUCIA CHASE—ballet dancer; founded American Ballet Theatre

CHARLES EDWARD IVES—composer; won Pulitzer Prize in music

GEORGE DURRIE—landscape painter; many of his paintings became Currier and Ives prints, painted *Home for Thanksgiving*

ROSA PONSELLE, EILEEN FARRELL—opera singers

JOHN KENSETT—artist, landscape painter

FREDERICK LAW OLMSTED—landscape architect; designed Central Park in New York City

AL CAPP—cartoonist, creator of "L'il Abner" and "Fearless Fosdick"

Very Important People

HENRY WARD BEECHER—clergyman; wrote *Aids to Prayer* and *Life of Jesus Christ*

EDWARD CALVIN KENDALL—scientist, Nobel Prize winner

JULES DASSIN—movie producer and director

UNCAS—chief of Mohegan Indian tribe; fought with colonists against Pequots; was the inspiration for Uncas in *Last of the Mohicans* written by James Fenimore Cooper

ETHAN ALLEN—Revolutionary War soldier

P.T. BARNUM—showman; helped create Ringling Brothers Barnum and Bailey Circus

JOHN BROWN—abolitionist

COLLIS P. HUNTINGTON—financier, railroad builder; helped create the Southern Pacific Railroad

ISRAEL PUTNAM—farmer, soldier, major general in Continental army; remembered for shouting, "Don't fire until you see the whites of their eyes!" at the Battle of Bunker Hill

More VIPs

JONATHAN EDWARDS—clergyman; wrote sermons that led to religious revival in colonial days known as the Great Awakening

ISAAC HULL—naval officer, commander of USS *Constitution* ("Old Ironsides")

ROGER LUDLOW—magistrate, one of the founders of the Connecticut Colony; presided over Connecticut's first court

BARBARA McCLINTOCK—biologist; won Nobel Prize in medicine for discovering genes can move around in chromosomes

J.P. MORGAN—financier; helped create U.S. Steel Corporation and other companies, donated valuable artwork and books to museums and libraries

NORMAN LEAR—television producer

ALBERT FULLER—founded Fuller Brush Company; started by selling brushes he made door to door

TAPPING REEVE—jurist, educator; founded Litchfield Law School, the first law school in the nation; started a movement to give women equal property rights

BENJAMIN SPOCK—physician, educator; wrote *Baby and Child Care*

GOOD GUYS

Elihu Yale was an English philanthropist who gave books and other items of value to the Collegiate School of Connecticut. In his honor, the school was later named Yale University.

Thomas Hopkins Gallaudet was an educator who founded the first free school for the deaf in America.

Ralph Nader is a consumer advocate who fights government and big business interests. He has taken on the automobile, coal, and meat industries to help inform, educate, and protect the American public. Nader ran as the Green Party presidential candidate in 2000 and garnered three percent of the popular vote.

BAD GUY

Benedict Arnold was an American soldier during the Revolutionary War. He served as a general, but later sided with the British and betrayed the colonies. He led the British to victory at Fort Trumbull and Fort Griswold.

Political Leaders

Dean Acheson–lawyer, statesman, U.S. secretary of state; won Pulitzer Prize in history

Ella Grasso–first woman to be elected governor in her own right, not to fill husband's term

Abraham Ribicoff–U.S. representative, governor, U.S. senator

Thomas Dodd–politician, U.S. representative, U.S. senator

Oliver Ellsworth–politician, chief justice of U.S. Supreme Court

Stephen Field–jurist, associate justice of U.S. Supreme Court

Roger Sherman–statesman, only American to sign the Articles of Association, Declaration of Independence, Articles of Confederation, and the U.S. Constitution; presented the Connecticut Compromise at the Constitutional Convention, U.S. representative, U.S. senator

John J. Sirica–jurist; presided over Watergate break-in trial

Lowell Palmer Weicker, Jr.–U.S. representative, U.S. senator

Morgan Bulkeley–first president of professional baseball's National League, governor of Connecticut, U.S. senator

George Murphy–actor, politician, U.S. senator

Joe Lieberman–politician, U.S. senator, first Orthodox Jew to run for vice-president

Keeping the Faith

Congregational Church, Southington–built in 1828

Center Church, New Haven–a United Church of Christ; built in 1812

Trinity Episcopal Church, Branford

First Congregational Church, Old Lyme

Schools

Rock School, New Canaan–built in 1799

Nathan Hale Schoolhouse, East Haddam–schoolhouse where Nathan Hale taught school in 1773-1774; moved from its original location and restored

U.S. Coast Guard Academy, New London

Wesleyan University, Middletown–founded in 1831 by Methodists, nonsectarian

Yale University, New Haven–the state's oldest and most famous school for higher education

Historic Sites

• **Dinosaur State Park,** Rocky Hill–most notable historic site in the state, geodesic dome encloses 500 dinosaur tracks

• **Berlin Historic District**–encompasses 50 18th- and 19th-century houses

• **Massacoh Plantation,** Simsbury–a preserved and restored collection of 18th- and 19th-century buildings, includes an old schoolhouse, tavern, manufacturing shop, and meeting house

• **Old New–Gate Prison National Historic Landmark,** East Granby–copper was discovered here in 1707; after the mine closed in 1773, it was converted to a prison

• **Putnam Memorial State Park,** Redding–the U.S. Continental Army had a winter camp here in 1778-1779; the 183-acre (74-hectare) park includes a small museum and a reconstructed blockhouse

• **Mount Riga Blast Furnace,** Salisbury–built around 1810, stands on a 1,000-foot (304-meter) plateau, near a lake that supplied waterpower to operate its bellows and manufacture anchors for the navy during the War of 1812

• **Cannon Square,** Stonington–site where the Stonington militia successfully fought off the British in 1814

Early Residency

Old State House, Hartford–erected between 1792-1796

Mark Twain House, Hartford–part of Nook Farm, a 140-acre (56-hectare) neighborhood favored by writers; termed an "architectural extravaganza"

Harriet Beecher Stowe House, Hartford–adjacent to the Mark Twain house

Noah Webster House, West Hartford–house and museum that display some of his books and papers

Fyler House, Windsor–one of the oldest buildings in the state, dates back to 1640

Roseland Cottage, Woodstock–summer retreat built in 1846 for Henry Bowen; the cottage was originally painted purple, now it is pink!

Bates-Scofield Homestead, Darien–a restored 1736 farmhouse; features a kitchen and buttery, a weaving room, and a colonial herb garden

Lockwood-Mathews Mansion, Norwalk–built in 1864, this residence cost $1.2 million

Henry Whitfield House, Guilford–built in 1639, this house is the oldest stone house in New England

Gillette Castle, Essex–home of actor and playwright William Gillette; an eccentric "castle" overlooking the Connecticut River, it took five years to complete (1914-1919)

A few of Connecticut's famous Battles

Battle of Sachem's Head, Leete's Island, near Branford–site of a bloody battle during the Pequot War in 1637

Mystic Battle–battle between Connecticut settlers and the Pequot Indians in 1637

Battle at Fort Shantok, near Uncasville–battle between the Mohegan and the Narragansett Indians

Fort Griswold Battle, Groton–major battle of the American Revolution

A few of Connecticut's Forts

Black Rock Fort, New Haven–Revolutionary War era

Fort Nathan Hale, New Haven–Civil War era

Fort Griswold, Groton–site of the most heroic, and tragic, battle of the Revolution

Libraries

Check out the following special state libraries! (Do you have a library card? Have you worn it out yet?!)

The Connecticut State Library, Hartford

Yale University Library, New Haven

The University of Connecticut Library, Storrs

Trinity College Library, Hartford

Wesleyan University Library, Middletown

Attractions

Beardsley Zoo, Bridgeport

Brookfield Craft Center, Brookfield

National Audubon Society, Greenwich

Hungerford Outdoor Education Center, Kensington

Lutz Children's Museum, Manchester

Mystic Marinelife Aquarium, Mystic

Hidden Valley Nature Center, New Fairfield

Marsh Botanical Garden, New Haven

Thames Science Center, New London

Mystic Seaport is the pride and joy of Connecticut. This recreated 19th-century seaport is a "living museum" where craftspeople practice the traditional crafts of the period. The 1841 whaling ship, the *Charles W. Morgan,* is a favorite exhibit. Another interesting exhibit is the replica of the *Amistad* slave ship. This replica was constructed in Mystic Seaport and made its maiden voyage in 2000. Be sure to check them out!

Museums

The Barnum Museum, Bridgeport–circus history museum

Discovery Museum, Bridgeport

American Clock and Watch Museum, Bristol

Military Museum of Southern New England, Danbury

Shore Line Trolley Museum, East Haven

Hill-Stead Museum, Farmington

Bruce Museum, Greenwich

Nautilus Memorial/Submarine Force Library & Museum, Groton

Eli Whitney Museum, Hamden

New Britain Youth Museum, New Britain

U.S. Coast Guard Museum, New London

Old Lighthouse Museum, Stonington

New England Air Museum, Windsor Locks

Peabody Museum of Natural History, New Haven

Monuments and Memorials

Charter Oak Memorial, Hartford

USS *Nautilus* Memorial, Groton–first nuclear-powered ship, this submarine was built in Groton and is now open to visitors

John Mason Monument, Mystic

Mark Twain Memorial, Hartford

The Arts

Goodspeed Opera House, East Haddam–puts on summer productions

Black Box Theatres, Trinity College–features plays and musicals

Yale Repertory Theater, New Haven

Long Wharf Theatre, New Haven

Shubert Theater, New Haven

Hartford Symphony Orchestra

National Theatre of the Deaf, Chester

Wadsworth Atheneum, Hartford–one of the nation's oldest art museums

Long Island Sound is at the southern border of Connecticut. Long Island, across the sound from most of the state, shelters the 253-mile (407-kilometer) Connecticut shoreline from most severe Atlantic storms. No place in the state is more than 75 miles (120 kilometers) from the Long Island Sound.

The New Haven Harbor Lighthouse is built of East Haven sandstone and lined with New Haven brick. The light was retired in 1877.

Roads...

Connecticut 169, from Canterbury to North Woodstock Lower Connecticut River Valley, loop from Middletown Litchfield Hills, Torrington loop

Bridges...

Middletown Bridge–crosses the state's longest river, the Connecticut River

...and more!

Valley Railroad Steam Train and Riverboat, Essex

Amtrak–provides passenger service along the shore through Hartford

Marshes and Estuaries

THE CONNECTICUT AUDUBON SOCIETY MAINTAINS A COASTAL CENTER ON A BARRIER BEACH AT MILFORD POINT. FROM THE BIRD SANCTUARY BOARDWALK, VISITORS CAN OBSERVE THE MARSHES. AN OBSERVATION TOWER NEARBY ALSO PROVIDES VIEWS OF THE MARSHES.

AN ESTUARY IS A BODY OF WATER WHERE FRESH WATER AND SALT WATER MIX. THE ESTUARY AT THE MOUTH OF THE HOUSATONIC RIVER IS MADE UP OF UPLANDS, TIDAL WETLANDS AND MUDFLATS, SAND SPITS AND BARRIER BEACHES, AND LONG ISLAND SOUND.

Animals of Connecticut

Connecticut's animals include:

Opossum
Otter
Rabbit
Skunk
White-tailed Deer

Beaver
Coyote
Fox
Mink
Muskrat

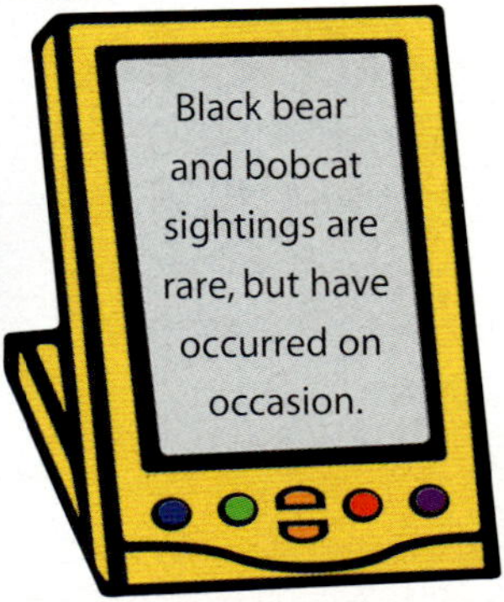

Some of Connecticut's endangered animals include:

Bald Eagle
Peregrine Falcon

Green Sea Turtle
Hawksbill Sea Turtle
Kemp's Turtle
Leatherback Sea Turtle
Loggerhead Sea Turtle

Birds

Blue Jay
Bobwhite
Chickadee
Crow
Duck
Goldfinch
Goose
Grouse
Gull
Hawk
Nuthatch
Pheasant
Robin
Sandpiper
Snowy Owl
Sparrow
Tern
Vireo
Warbler
Woodcock
Woodpecker

Don't let these Connecticut bugs bug you!

Ants
Beetle
Bumblebee
Butterfly
Cicada
Cricket
Dragonfly
Firefly
Grasshopper
Honeybee
Katydid
Ladybug
Mayfly
Mosquito
Moth
Praying Mantis
Walking Stick
Weevil
Yellow Jacket

Butterfly

Dragonfly

Bumblebee

Ladybug

Fish

Swimming in Connecticut waters:

Blackfish
Bluefish
Bluegill
Brook Trout
Bullhead
Butterfish
Flounder
Perch
Pickerel
Scup
Sea Bass
Striped Bass

Sea Critters

In Connecticut's Coastal Waters, you may find:

- Bottlenose Dolphin
- Blue Whale
- Clams
- Electric Ray
- Harbor Seal
- Humpback Whale
- Leatherback Turtle
- Right Whale
- Shark
- Skate
- Squid
- Sunfish

Bottlenose dolphins send messages to each other by whistling and squealing. They will help an injured dolphin get to the surface so it can breathe!

Seashells

She sells seashells by the seashore!

Bubble Shell
Cockle
Moon Shell
Mussel
Oyster
Periwinkle
Scallop
Shipworm
Slipper Shell
Top Shell
Vampire Shell
Wentletrap
Whelk

Top Shells got their names because their high, pointed shape makes them look like children's toy tops.

TREEMENDOUS!

THESE TREES GRACE THE STATE OF CONNECTICUT:

Ash
Basswood
Beech
Birch
Butternut
Hemlock
Hickory
Maple
Oak
Pine
Red Cedar

Flowers

Are you crazy about these Connecticut wildflowers?

- Bloodroot
- Buttercup
- Columbine
- Cowslip
- Jack-in-the-Pulpit
- Lady's Slipper
- Lupine
- Milkweed
- Spring Beauty
- Violet
- Wild Geranium

Cream of the Crops

Connecticut's agricultural products include:

Sweet Corn

Potatoes

Apples

Tobacco

Hay

Sheep

Chickens &
Eggs

Beef Cattle

Connecticut Potpourri

Connecticut has the highest average annual paycheck in the nation.

Connecticut has the highest percentage of people with college degrees.

Hartford is known as America's insurance capital.

New Haven claims to be the home of the first hamburger and the first pizza sold in the United States.

Danbury is known as Hat City. The Stetson, or "10-gallon hat," was first made here.

Connecticut has the lowest poverty rate in the nation.

Festivals

U.S. Eastern Ski Jumping Championships, Salisbury–held in February

Dogwood Festival, Fairfield–held in May

Lobster Weekend, Mystic–held in May

Jazz Festival, New Haven–held in July

Barnum Festival, Bridgeport–held in July

Native American Festival, Haddam–held in August

Norwalk Oyster Festival–held in September

Fall New Haven Antiques Show –held in September

Christmas Torchlight Parade, Old Saybrook–held in December

Holidays Calendar

- Martin Luther King, Jr. Day, *3rd Monday in January*
- Presidents' Day, *3rd Monday in February*
- St. Patrick's Day, *March 17*
- Memorial Day, *last Monday in May*
- Independence Day, *July 4*
- Columbus Day, *2nd Monday in October*
- Veterans Day, *November 11*
- Thanksgiving, *4th Thursday in November*
- Christmas, *December 25*

September 17 marks the anniversary of the U.S. Constitution. On this date in 1787, delegates from 12 states—including Connecticut—met at the Constitutional Convention in Philadelphia, Pennsylvania. They voted unanimously to approve this most important document.

Connecticut's Fabulous Food!

- Fried Clam Bellies
- Steamed Clams
- Thin-crust Pizza
- Apple Cobbler
- Clam Chowder
- Corn-on-the-Cob

Connecticut Works!

Many of America's largest corporations are based in Connecticut. Financial firms and service industries are as important as manufacturing and trade. Connecticut manufactures transportation equipment, machinery, chemicals, food products, and much more.

Much of the state's wholesale and retail trade is domestic since Connecticut is located in a densely populated region. This region makes up one of the richest consumer and industrial markets in the United States. The three ports that handle any foreign trade are New Haven, Bridgeport, and New London.

State Books & Websites

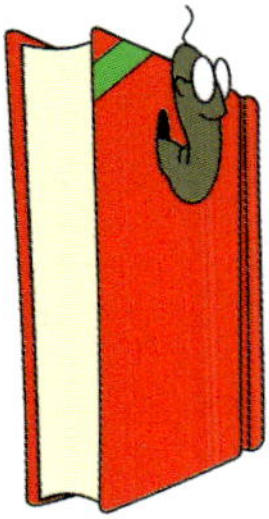

My First Book About Connecticut by Carole Marsh

America the Beautiful: Connecticut by Sylvia McNair

Let's Discover the States: Connecticut by the Aylesworths

The Connecticut Experience Series by Carole Marsh

Connecticut Glossary

GLOSSARY WORDS

abolitionist: a person opposed to slavery

azure: the blue of a clear, unclouded sky

constitution: a document outlining the role of a government

emancipation: to be set free

immigrant: a person who comes to a new country to live

indentured: to work for someone for a set period of time in exchange for something

revolution: the overthrow of a government

secede: to voluntarily give up being a part of an organized group

Yankee: nickname used by Dutch sailors for English settlers; patriots adopted the name and began calling themselves Yankees during the Revolutionary War

Connecticut Spelling Bee

Here are some special Connecticut-related words to learn! To take the Spelling Bee, have someone call out the words and you spell them aloud or write them on a piece of paper. Good luck!

Spelling Words

Appalachian	Nautilus
Connecticut	Nutmeggers
Hartford	Pequot
Housatonic	provisions
Litchfield	Quinnipiac
Mashantucket	Uncasville
Massacoe	Willimantic
Naugatuck	Yankee

About the Author

ABOUT THE AUTHOR...

CAROLE MARSH has been writing about Connecticut for more than 20 years. She is the author of the popular Connecticut State Stuff series for young readers and creator, along with her son, Michael Marsh, of "Connecticut Facts and Factivities," a CD-ROM widely used in Connecticut schools. The author of more than 100 Connecticut books and other supplementary educational materials on the state, Marsh is currently working on a new collection of Connecticut materials for young people. Marsh correlates her Connecticut materials to the Connecticut Common Core of Learning standards. Many of her books and other materials have been inspired by or requested by Connecticut teachers and librarians.

EDITORIAL ASSISTANTS...

Terry Briggs

Jill Sanders

Billie Walburn